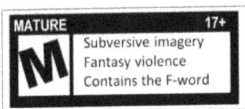

I0202455

MATURE 17+
M
Subversive imagery
Fantasy violence
Contains the F-word

– What if there was an equation that could tell you what to do?

In this dog-eat-dog world of office politics that keeps us shivering like frightened squirrels at our cubicles, enhanced productivity techniques are essential. The only problem is finding out about them before others do. Well, here is your chance. Welcome to the world of Time management design, your survival guide for the irritations and potential humiliations of the modern workplace.

The promise of Time management design is this: You can find refuge while hitting your goals and achieving more than you ever thought possible while also enjoying what you do in spite of the constantly elevating constraints from a sometimes clueless management. Finally, a "blue ocean strategy" for workers is emblazoned in this anti-authoritarian and subversive business book. *Steal it!*

This book is for:
- managers trying to increase the performance of their teams,
- HR personnel trying to simplify the employee review process, and, most of all,
- workers trying to ease themselves from the rat race by employing stealth methods to stay ahead of the pack with less effort.

# Time Management Design

- Applying analytical techniques to improve work habits and increase personal productivity
- By Michael Kotas

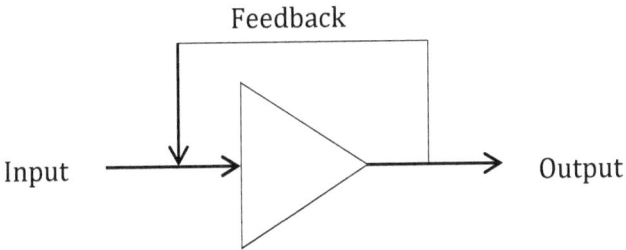

Feedback

Input → Output

Bags Press
Tucson, AZ

Cataloging Data:

Kotas, Michael
      Time Management Design: Applying analytical techniques to improve work habits and increase personal productivity / Michael Kotas
1 Business—Humor I Title
First edition, September 2012

Bags Press
ISBN-13: 978-0615676623 (Custom Universal)
ISBN-10: 0615676626

# Dedication

To my wife Julia who took a full time job so that I could take a sabbatical and write about work.

And to my late parents, Geraldine and Norbert Kotas, who ingrained in me empathy, honesty and a work ethic that I can't seem to shake.

Also, to all the great managers and mentors who have helped me in my career: I'll be dissing a lot of people in this book, you are not among them.

# Contents

"The mind is sharper and keener in seclusion and uninterrupted solitude. No big laboratory is needed in which to think. Originality thrives in seclusion free of outside influences beating upon us to cripple the creative mind. Be alone, that is the secret of invention; be alone, that is when ideas are born." – Nikola Tesla

# Preface

Facebook CEO Mark Zuckerberg has famously pointed out that an exceptional employee can produce as much as one hundred times the output of an ordinary employee. Which begs the questions: *How do they get that way? Is it possible for an ordinary employee to become an exceptional employee?* The answer to these questions is the subject of this book—the author presents a mathematical basis for determining the best use of one's time.

Many organizations grapple with the question: *"What should our employees do?"* And employees, striving to get ahead, ask themselves: *"What should we do?"* Rightfully so—the more you do, the more you are worth in this (supposedly) meritocratic society. And who doesn't want to be worth more?

But, how do you go about it?

It turns out the answer is not so complicated. For the first time an analytical approach to time management is revealed. The method applies not only to business people, engineers, and academics but also to creative types, artists, and people in all fields with complex jobs.

So, get ready for a surprise—the application of some straightforward mathematics paves the way to answering one of the great questions of our time: *"What the f\*\*k should I do?"*

# Chapter One

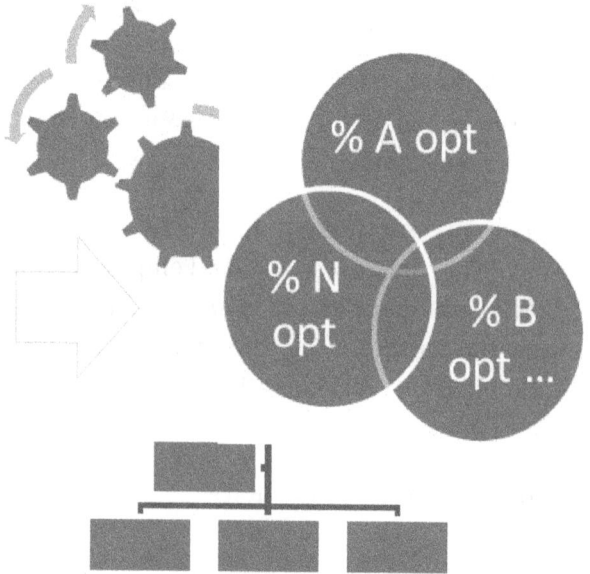

Time management design: Where

have you been all my life?

# So, you're stuck in a cube farm and your boss is an asshole

- Your situation is hopeless, right?
- Not as long as you are holding this book in your hot little hands.

The promise of Time management design is this: There is a place you can go to find freedom and refuge from the workaday world and escape the monotony and drudgery of your job. You can crack open a vast space and accomplish more than you ever thought possible, hit your goals, and enjoy what you do in spite of the constantly expanding constraints by a sometimes clueless management.

Borrowing ideas from technologists, we will unlock powerful tools to understand and evaluate your work, what you do, what other people tell you to do—and prove if they have a value or not.

Let's face it, there is a lot that goes on in an office that you'd rather not be a part of. I hasten to add that you'd rather be just about any other place on earth. But there you are five days a week, eight hours a day (if you're lucky)—all the while telling yourself it's not so bad being chained to your Crackberry.

What to do?

Answer: Discover a personal oasis by increasing your capacity to work smarter.

# You are a slave

- The world has conspired against you.

As Morpheus so eloquently pointed out in *The Matrix*, "You are a slave." Just as it took Neo the entire movie to understand his place in the Matrix before blasting off from a telephone booth, an oracle of sorts will need to unveil your eyes—me!

Now, you are Neo. As that movie ends, so this book begins. Learning the secrets to the Matrix would only imply that you are a battery—you are about to learn the world of stealthy operations within the workplace. You'll be one step ahead of your conspiring co-workers—your strategies will make you more productive and fawned upon by management.

The irony is that these techniques are not mystical or obscure but rather practical implementations of well-known principles. In effect, you will be conspiring with powerful forces for getting things done. (Have I heard that somewhere before?)

# The bitter irony

> – You want your life to be easy. Everyone else is working to make it harder.

Do not let my worldview distract you from what is worthwhile in this book, but I believe that in business there is an "us-against-them mentality." The ideas explained here are the outcomes of many years incubating ideas alone. I had the luxury of working for fifteen years in a home office—trained in engineering principles, I could apply them to my job in technical sales without the distractions of office politics.

I believe the "us-against-them mentality" that governs the workplace is a fact that makes the use of enhanced productivity tools essential. You are competing against your co-workers and being judged by people with flawed ways of thinking; you are trapped in other peoples' worlds and their ways of doing things. You can either convince them that they are wrong (good luck) or succeed in spite of them.

The fact is the world is your oyster if you only get a little leverage on the right problems.

This book will reveal secrets that can help you deal with the dullards with whom you must interact, teach you how to deal with them (or not deal with them), and streamline your workload, improve your performance, and feel better about yourself.

# Time management design: Where have you been all my life?

I googled "time management design" and up popped the usual suspects, 517 million of them in .24 seconds, but none actually contained the words "time management design" (except a Word document template). I searched Network Solutions and absconded with the domain name, "time management design.com."

I had to admit I was surprised to find that two major concepts in business and culture: time management and design, did not seem to be combined previously. But as this was the subject of my upcoming book—I was OK with it.

To summarize the approach: We will be applying design principles, in the technical sense, to time management using analytical methods based on mathematics.

- Companies don't value what is important.
- Exit the rat race for good.

Business is not funny. In fact, businesses have lost their way. Corporations are all about being serious. Take a rubber chicken or whoopee cushion to the next company meeting and you will find out that companies do not value what is important.

The world is full of iPhone addled posers flying around acting important. You can't smother them with an airline pillow (those disappeared long ago); why it's hard enough just to ignore them. Once I saw a guy cutting his nose hairs while waiting in line for a Southwest flight. These people have no idea that karma is about to catch up with them.

They will get theirs. Ultimately, their phony posturing will melt into irrelevance as you rise to a higher place. Take refuge in the clear, flowing stream of the principles of Time management design and dispense with these fools. Exit the rat race for good.

# Stealthy operations

- Don't let them know what you're doing.

Being stealthy may seem like a blatant discrepancy with the basic tenets of transparency, but it's not. Your job, your work, your knowledge should be transparent. To you. Not necessarily to anyone else.

You must not let them know what you are doing. You must carry secrets about your latest activities, plans, and goals in order to stay ahead of the pack.

That is not a problem, because if you are implementing the principles in this book, your managers will be happy as clams.

# Control their expectations

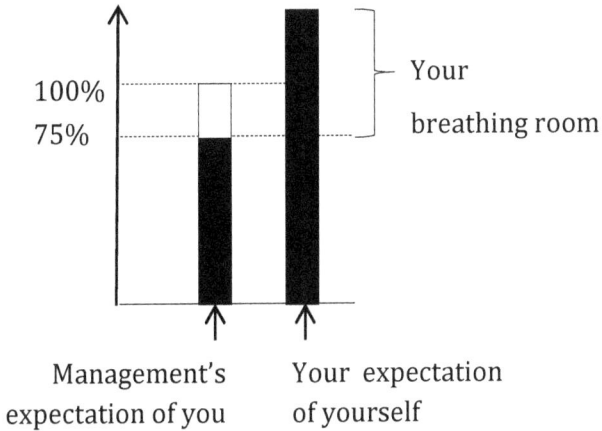

100%

75%

Your

breathing room

Management's
expectation of you

Your expectation
of yourself

Another reason why it's important to be stealthy is that you don't want to raise expectations unnecessarily. This simple fact is well known to anyone in sales. If you create an environment in which management has the same expectations of you as you have for yourself, it is a recipe for failure. Your expectations should always be higher than theirs.

The graph above demonstrates this principle. The bar chart on the left represents your manager's expectations for you. Typically, they will want to raise their expectations (for you, not for themselves) such that they really only expect you to achieve about 75 percent of what they tell you they want.

By association, everything you tell them will go into the category of possibilities that they see for you. So it makes no sense to tell them. The space between 100 percent of your expectations and 75 percent of their expectations is your "breathing room."

# How I know this

- My background in experimental fluid mechanics
- Ludwig von Rochau and the Realpolitik of business

Once a venture capitalist-type at the company I worked for paid me the highest compliment by saying that I applied principles of engineering to sales. And he was right. But I never thought about it much because I assumed everybody did. Time management design (TMD) is an analytical method based on principles employed in scientific research. The main mathematical operation is correlation, which is commonly used in experiments.

Time management design also employs feedback, an amplification device. Together with evaluation (using correlation), these provide the two governing principles. I knew about feedback from my background in experimental fluid mechanics and specifically from using a hot wire anemometer. These are basic concepts in that field.

In my career, I have had the chance to work for many different companies. I divined the commonalities across organizations—what they did well and what they did not so well—and developed Realpolitikal views[1] about business: "Most companies succeed in spite of themselves." I observed that organizations are dysfunctional and have at their core the need to perpetuate bad ideas, promote yes-men, reward mediocrity, etc.

Working from my home and being in an incubator of sorts, allowed me to see what others, immersed in bad situations, could not or would not see.

*"But, thar's gold in them hills!"* By implementing the ideas contained here—subversive, dysfunctional or otherwise—you will literally be handed the *"keys to the Kingdom."* Your work will improve. You will be happier and get more done.

---

[1] Ludwig von Rochau, a German writer and politician in the 19th century, coined the term "Realpolitik." His 1853 book *Grundsätze der Realpolitik angewendet auf die staatlichen Zustände Deutschlands* describes the meaning of the term.

# Design

## – What is design?

If you ask an engineer and a regular person, "What is design?" you will probably get two different answers. Most nontechnical people think design is a noun, related to the appearance of something whereas engineers and technical people know that design is actually a verb, relating to a process. To design something does not mean "to make it look cool" but to optimize a result based on multiple (usually conflicting) parameters, such as cost vs. performance or speed vs. weight.

OK, engineers are nerds.

I'm not saying that design is not appreciated or understood in the nontechnical world, I just want to clarify that design is based on mathematical procedures, and this is the approach we will take in this book.

Time management design is a mathematical process.

```
              Feedback
         ┌──────────────┐
         │              │
         ↓         ╱│
Input ──────→   ╱  │
              ╱    │───────→   Output
              ╲    │
                ╲  │
                  ╲│
```

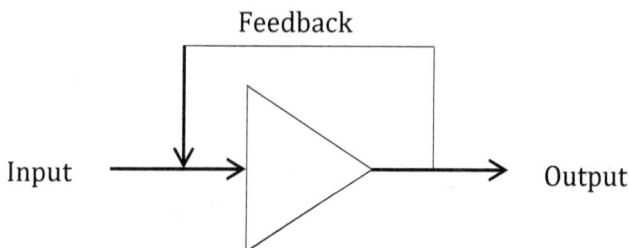

Above is a diagram of a feedback loop. Note: the output goes back into the input, thus *feedback*. Feedback in a microphone occurs when the output (from the speaker) goes back into the microphone (the input) thus making a loud, unpleasant noise.

But, of course you knew that, right??

# What you should do

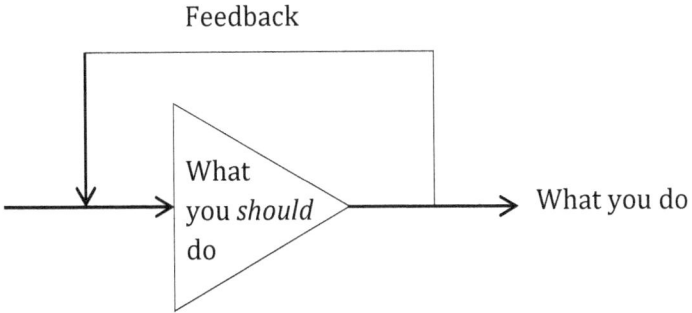

This book is about closing the gap between what you do, and what you *should* do.

We are going to close the gap using feedback and self-evaluation. By understanding the mechanisms affecting the output, you will be able to condition the input to further increase (or decrease) the output. The result is a powerful engine of optimization providing efficiency gains and clear thinking.

# Chapter Two

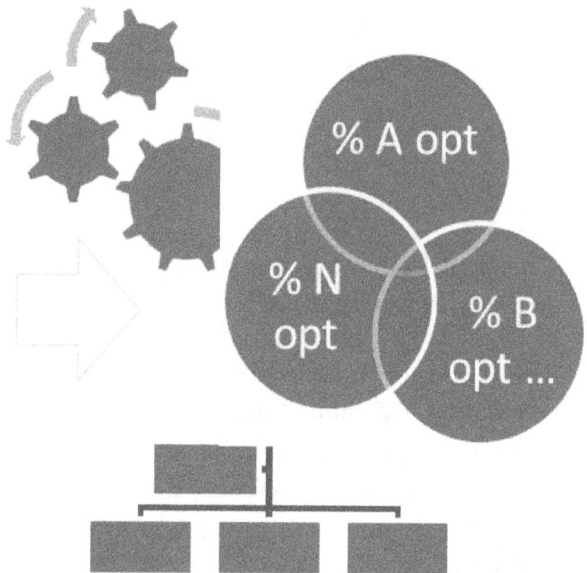

# The Principles of Time management

# design

# A clown at a circus

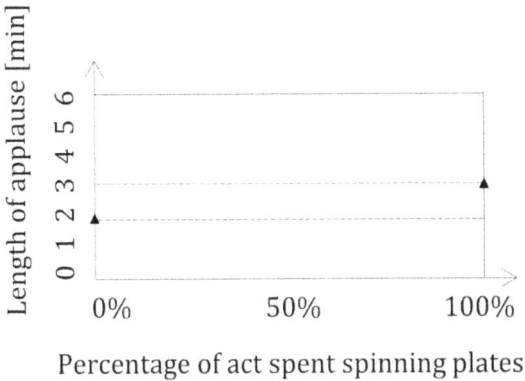

Percentage of act spent spinning plates

To understand the principle of Time management design, we begin with a simple example. Imagine you are a clown at a circus. Your goal is to entertain the crowd, thus keeping your job or making more money. Unfortunately, you only know how to do two things: spin plates and tame a lion.

You have a measure of the crowd's entertainment: the total length (duration) of applause. If you just spin plates, you receive three minutes of applause whereas if you tame the lion for the whole act, you receive two minutes. What happens if you combine plate spinning with lion taming—will it increase the crowd's entertainment?

The exercise is represented on the chart, with Length of applause vs. Percentage of act spent spinning plates. (We could have used Percentage of act spent taming lion, but these always sum to 100%).

The known data is: L = 3 at 100% plate spinning and L = 2 at 0% (100% lion taming). What is the behavior away from the end points? How can we obtain it? Is it true that that combining plate spinning and lion taming increases entertainment? If so, where is entertainment optimized?

# Clown data

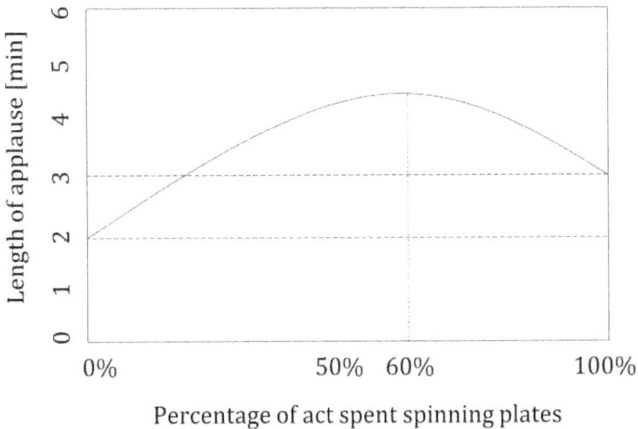

Percentage of act spent spinning plates

To answer these questions, the clown repeats his act several times each time changing the value of Percentage of act spent spinning plates.

He carries out the act for 10 percent plate spinning (90 percent lion taming), 20 percent plate spinning, etc., each time measuring the total duration of applause.

The result is the curve above and with it, the clown has the answers to his questions. Yes, combining plate spinning and lion taming increases entertainment. Entertainment is optimized at 60 percent plate spinning. The highest value of applause is more than four minutes.

The clown has all the information he needs to advance his career and earn more money.

Unfortunately, he was fired anyway.

# The problem

- How do you know you are doing
  the right things?

The clown example illuminates the problem: "How do you know you are doing the right things?"

Time management design provides the answer via the process of optimizing a set of tasks. Some aspects of the clown's job cannot be reproduced in an office setting (good luck with the applause) but some can. Most jobs have an arbitrary set of activities, a goal, and the means of varying the activities to influence the goal. In this regard, the gist of the clown's experiment can be reproduced in the workplace.

And so we shall. What follows is a mathematical method for optimizing a set of tasks employing self-evaluation and feedback.

# Percentage activities chart

- Time management design is the process of optimizing the size of the Percentage activity areas.

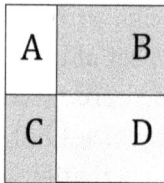

|   |   |
|---|---|
| A | B |
| C | D |

We begin by representing the sum of all activities by a "percentage activities chart," which is a square pie chart (please don't ask me why it's square) representing the percentage of time spent on each activity by its proportional area. % A + % B + ... % N = 100%

If % A ini is some initial guess as to the optimum size of Percentage activity area A and % A opt is the optimum size, then the problem is reduced to finding % A opt, % B opt ... % N opt.

# Representation by time series

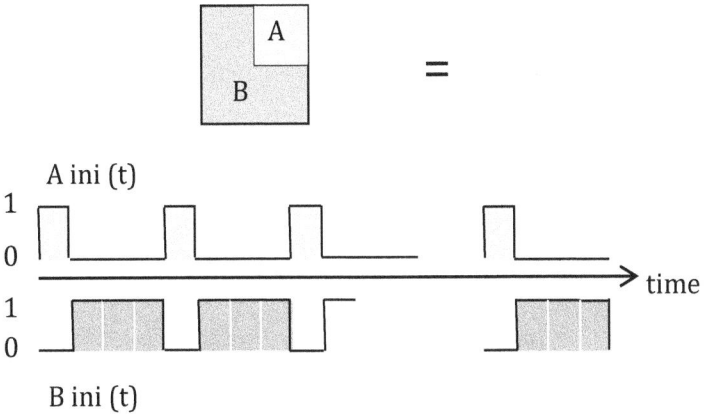

The Percentage activities chart represents the proportion of time spent on a set of activities. The same proportion exists when the data is plotted as a time series, as shown above.

For the Percentage activities chart shown, with two activities, % A ini= 25% and % B ini = 75%, a time series representing A ini (t) and B ini (t) is shown.

Logic 1 represents the time Activity A is carried out, and Logic 0 when it is not. For each unit spent on A, three units are spent on B or % A = $\frac{A}{A+B}$ = $\frac{1}{1+3}$ = 25%.

# Fractional activity, $R_A$

- Change the percentage of time spent on A and see how it affects the system.

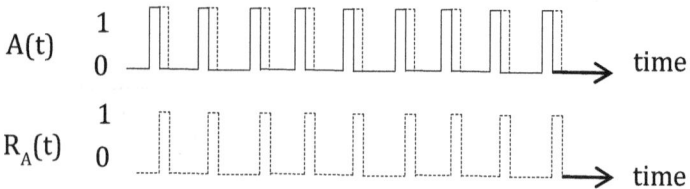

Fractional activity, $R_A(t) = A(t) - A\,ini\,(t)$

In order to find out the relative importance of activities, we need to vary them. This is done by arbitrarily increasing or decreasing the amount of time spent on an activity and isolating the variation using subtraction.

Consider the time series above. Activity A(t) is represented as the combination of a dotted and a solid line. The solid line corresponds to A ini, the dotted line to some arbitrarily additional amount of A.

Now subtract A ini from A(t) to produce the dotted line contribution only. We call this time series, "Fractional activity," as it corresponds to some fractional increase or decrease from the initital value. Fractional activity,

$R_A(t)$ is defined as that part of the time series during which Percentage activity exceeds the initial value, i.e.

$$R_A(t) = A\,(t) - A\,\text{ini}\,(t)$$

Similarly, Fractional activity B, $R_B$, represents the deviation of B from % B ini, etc.

# The goal metric

- characteristics of the ideal
  goal metric

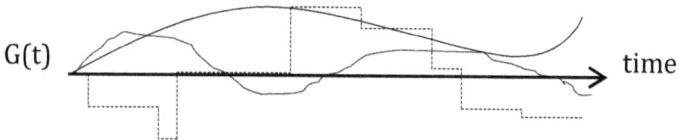

G(t)                                                                 time

What we have established with Fractional activity is a way to vary activities (from some initial value) without the need to repeat the task (as in the clown example). This allows us to evaluate the effect of changing activities in real time. Next, like in the clown example, we need to find a suitable goal metric.

In business, it would be nice to use a goal metric such as revenue, EBITDA, or something similar. For reasons that may be obvious and will be spelled out later, such goal metrics are typically not suitable.

For our purposes, the ideal goal metric has the following characteristics: 1) is related to the activities being performed (otherwise, what is the point?), 2) is continuous (or, at least, *continuously available* for sampling), and 3) has good variability (for purposes of "robustness," or "dynamic range").

Let's leave the discussion about possible goal metrics until the next chapter. In the following we assume that the goal metric has the above properties.

# Correlation

$$C(R_A, G) = \frac{1}{T} \int_0^T R_A(t) * G(t)dt$$

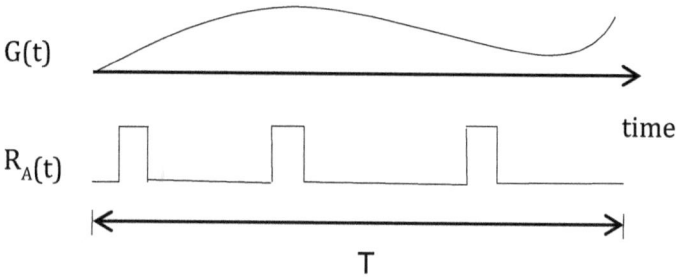

In time series analysis, the relationship between two variables is calculated using the mathematical operation, *correlation*. Correlation, as the name implies, is a measure of how well correlated (or uncorrelated) two series are.

For the two time series shown: Fractional activity, $R_A(t)$, and goal metric, $G(t)$, the correlation , $C(R_A, G)$, is given by:

$$C(R_A, G) = \frac{1}{T} \int_0^T R_A(t) * G(t)dt$$

Which means: to calculate the correlation, multiply $R_A$ and G during the interval T and then divide by T. In other words, take the average of the product. (If you want to convince yourself that this actually does produce a measure of correlation, see: *Appendix 2*).

The really important thing about C is that:

- C is positive when % A ini < % A opt (is less than the optimum value),
- C is negative when % A ini > % A opt (is greater than the optimum value), and
- C = 0 when % A ini is equal to % A opt.

In other words, $C(R_A,G)$ shows if the Percentage activity area A is too big, too small, or "just right," which is exactly what we need.

# Out-of-balance indicator

- C serves as an "error condition"

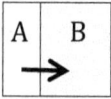

% A too small

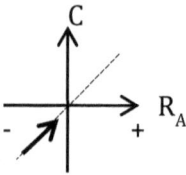

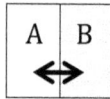

% A just right

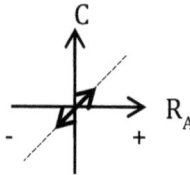

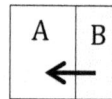

% A too big

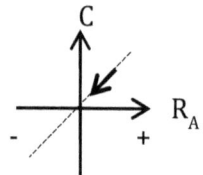

Let us take a closer look at the properties of the correlation function, $C(R_A,G)$.

For a work process with two activities, optimized at % A opt = % B opt = 50% (shown above) we can have only three cases: 1) % A ini is too small (left), 2) % A ini is too big (right), or 3) % A ini is "just right" (middle). For these three cases, the behavior of C vs. $R_A$ is shown. [1]

The left hand chart illustrates the case in which Activity A isn't performed enough; the proportional area is too small. Increasing the amount causes the goal to go up and therefore produces a correlation (with negative sign). The right hand chart illustrates the opposite case in which doing less of Activity A is positively correlated with the goal. The sign of the correlation indicates that Activity A is performed too much. In the case where % A is "just right" (center), the goal has a local maximum—doing more or less of it causes the goal to go down. This is explained in more detail in Appendix 2.

Note that the sign of the correlation indicates whether to do more or less of an activity and, therefore, acts as a kind of "error condition." Knowing whether the Percentage activity area A is too big, too small, or just right is equivalent to the clown finding out that entertainment is optimized at the Percentage of act spent spinning plates equals 60 percent—with the important difference that it can be applied in real time and used to modify work procedures "dynamically."

We have here assumed knowledge of % A opt in order to show that the out-of-balance indicator identifies the optimum state. When used with an unknown percentage activities chart, the out-of-balance indicator will determine the optimum state. Therefore, C has the characteristics required for a feedback signal.

---

[1] The shape of C vs. $R_A$ depends on the shape of G vs. % A (see Appendix 2). We have used a typical case.

# Block diagram of a work process

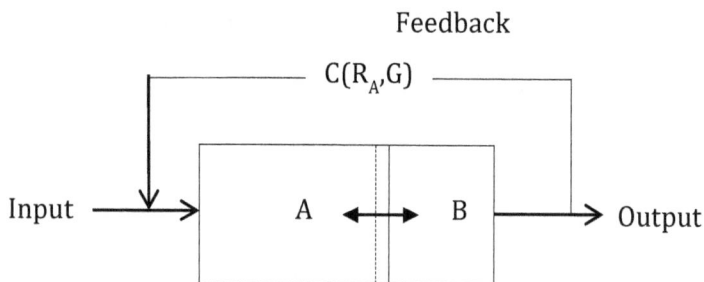

Feedback

$$C(R_A,G)$$

Input $\longrightarrow$ A $\longleftrightarrow$ B $\longrightarrow$ Output

We have all the necessary parts to optimize a work process: 1) a time series modified to vary percentage activities, 2) a goal metric, and 3) the means to correlate the two. This is illustrated in the above block diagram. The procedure to perform Time management design can thus be summarized: vary % A, isolate the variation, correlate with a goal metric, and use the error condition, C, to "push" % Activity area A to an optimum state. Repeat for B, C, D ... N.

- a statement of management's job in the form of an explicit equation

$$C_N(R_A, G) = \sum_1^N \frac{1}{T} \int_0^T R_A(t) * G(t)dt$$

Since we have an equation that expresses the objective of a single worker, it is trivial to generalize to an entire workforce. And who can resist?

If a single worker's objective is to maximize the goal metric, the sum over all workers expresses the objective of the board of directors, the CEO, your boss, his boss, etc. Simply by placing an additional sum in front of the previous equation and summing over all the members of the organization or "team," N, yields an equation for management's job, i.e. *"Go find where $C_N = 0$, bee-atch!"*

In most cases, people will look at this equation, understand the implications on the data and record keeping requirements, and dispense with it. Does that mean it is not valid to treat work as data? Absolutely not. It only means that most companies are far behind in implementing the tools that will help them get ahead.

# Conclusion

- We have solved the problem:
  "What should we do?"

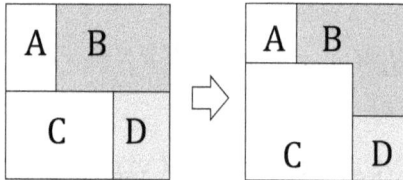

| % A ini, | % A opt, |
| % B ini ... | % B opt ... |
| % N ini | % N opt |

We have established a technique to optimize percentage activities. In principle, we have answered the question: "What should I do?" The next step is to show that implementing Time management design not only optimizes activities but also increases productivity allowing you to float effortlessly to that place Dorothy arrived after clicking her heals three times. No, not Kansas.

# Chapter Three

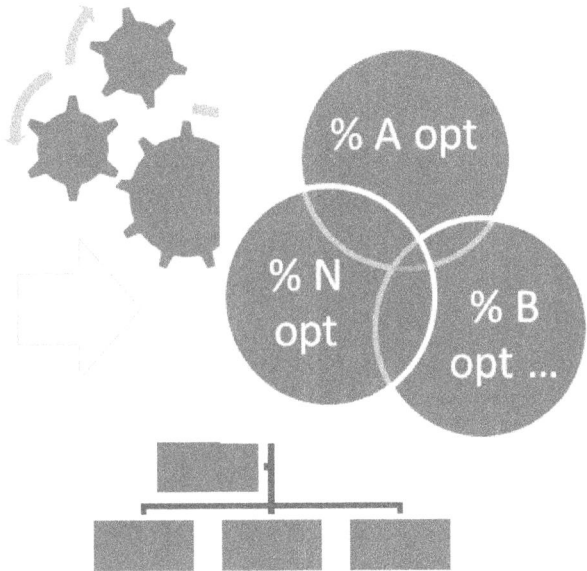

# Implementing Time management design

# Got skepticism?

- The goal metric is contaminated by multiple contributions and has a time scale and intermittency that renders it dubious
- and there are other problems.

In the previous chapter, we developed a tool for optimizing the time spent on an arbitrary group of activities. The astute businessman or woman has probably thought of many reasons why this technique either won't work or would be incredibly difficult to implement.

Such reasons could include the following.

1) Logging time spent on activities is itself counterproductive; producing a useful measure of "fractional activity" (are you kidding?) is unrealistic.

2) Activities can be interdependent: failing to do one can impact others. Tracking all the complex relations between different types of activities is cumbersome at best and could do more harm than good.

3) The duration of an activity is not a direct measure of its power to produce results.

4) Most useful goals (earnings, revenue, etc.) are the result of contributions due to many people and don't represent an individual's performance. In addition, most useful goals are intermittent, stochastic, or change over long periods of time and therefore are not correlated with activities.

In short, it appears that Time management design although possibly correct in theory has so many problems in implementation as to render it useless or even counter-productive.

But such is not the case! In this chapter, we consider these problems and demonstrate that implementing Time management design not only overcomes them but actually generates additional benefits in the implementation.

We begin by considering a well-accepted business principle and how interpreting it in the context of Time management design principles presents some tantalizing and almost unbelievable implications.

# The 80- 20 Rule

- Reinterpreting the Pareto
  Principle in Time management
  design terms

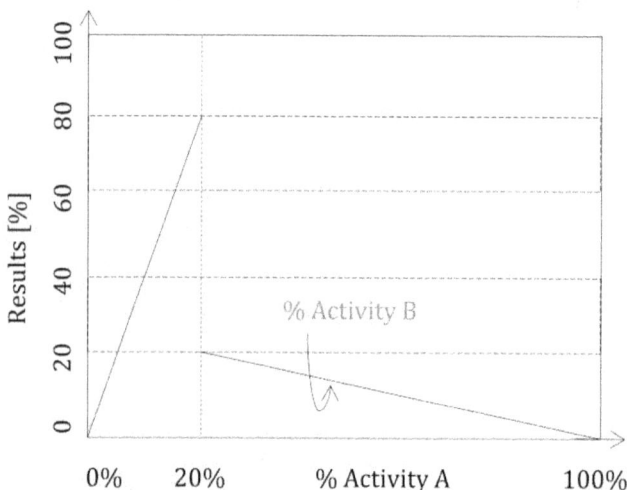

During the next employee review, try this. Tell your boss, "I've discovered that 20 percent of what I do produces 80 percent of the results!" See if you aren't, at the very least, severely reprimanded.

Even though the 80-20 Rule is commonly accepted, it presents such odd implications that most business people prefer not to acknowledge it. Yes, the implications of the 80-20 Rule are best kept under your hat.

Let's look at the 80-20 Rule in Time management design terms.

Above is our familiar chart, a goal metric vs. Percentage activity A. The 80-20 Rule states that some activity A produces 80 percent of the results, even though it is performed 20 percent of the time. By charting the data points and comparing the slope of the two curves we see that the slope of G(A) is 16 times the slope of G(B).

The implications are:

1) A marginal change in A is equivalent to 16 times B or for every additional A performed, the need to do 16 B is eliminated.

2) For each additional percent of A performed productivity increases by 4 percent.

3) Increasing % A is always associated with an increase in the goal metric until optimized at % A equals 100 percent at which point productivity has increased by 400 percent!

# Finding leverage

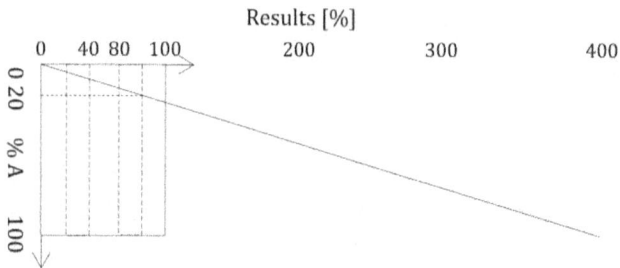

Extending the graph on the previous page illustrates the power of leveraging: the graph won't even fit on the page unless turned sideways! The Pareto Principle has so much support as to be an empirical fact. So use it.

Another way of looking at the 80 – 20 Rule is to acknowledge a vast potential in interpreting how the effect of what you do contributes to a goal.

The crux of the matter is that you need to be able to recognize these critical leveraging effects, whether they be comparisons in strategy, recognizing wasteful activities, determining the effects of different policies (or any type of abstract comparison between ideas, principles, tasks, etc.). The best way to identify such productivity levers is by implementing a technique based on real-time feedback and goal correlation.

# Tracking activity

- Problem: The duration of an activity is not a direct measure of its power to produce results.
- Solution: Map analog activities to digital outputs.

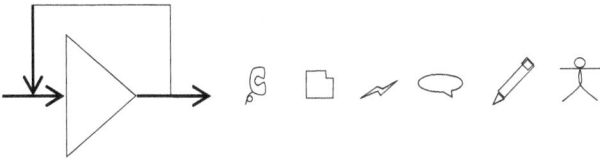

Before we get too excited let us return to another "flawed" concept of Time management design: using time to measure results.

 We are not clowns. The time it takes to do an activity is not linearly related to its output (and who can sit at their desk with a stopwatch?). On the contrary, if it is productivity we seek, the amount of time it takes to complete an activity should be decreased. That's clear: repetition, skill, experience all drive productivity higher.

So we will model not activity *per se*, but the "deliverable" of activity: output. For example, the output of the activity of "making a phone call" is a "completed phone call." The output of the activity of "writing an e-mail" is a "completed e-mail," etc. Instead of referring to Activities A, B, C, D, we shall speak of Outputs A, B, C, D, thus mapping *analog* activities to *digital* outputs.

Tracking outputs is more convenient than recording the time it takes to do something using the CRM system or old-fashioned spiral notebook.

Consider using icons to represent outputs (most CRM systems do not allow you to represent data graphically). Icons stand out from words and have the look and feel of data.

Personally, I use the following icons as the "deliverables" of activity:

Lightning bolt: e-mail sent

Pencil: document written

Telephone handset: message left

Stick figure: client met
Talk balloon: phone call made, etc.

How many phone calls did you make last week? Count the Talk balloons (or query the CRM).

Creative Idea: Develop your own icons and use them to track the output of activities.

- Get a bigger shelf.
- Get better tools.

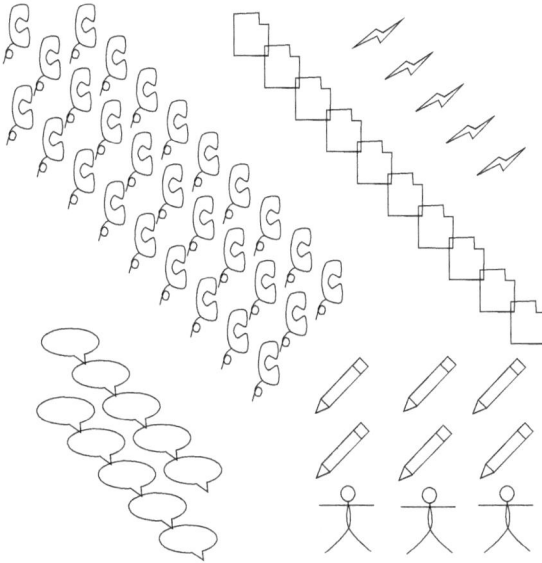

Icons help simplify and focus your activities as a classification device that enables measurement. Icons help increase your work capacity. Increasing your work capacity makes your job easier.

If you have too much stuff to fit on your shelf, what do you do? Get a bigger shelf. Consider your brain: Are the compartments too small? Increase their capacity. If the human mind can create dream worlds while sleeping, you can probably create better filing system.

Are the tools you are using insufficient? If so, get better tools. Do you know what tools will provide greater capacity? If not, do some research. Get new software, update your hardware, read about technology, and ask your friends and co-workers what they use.

Tools will do your work for you.

## Keyword your brain

You know what keywords are. You know what filing systems are. Think about what things have in common. Think about how you would classify the stuff you do. Create filing systems for your filing systems.

Want to be more creative? Ask: "What can I create."

# Mister Goodmetric

Time management design is unassailable: Input the data, and a result is certain (provided the right conditions are met). Any goal can be used, however some are better than others. Recall, the ideal properties of the goal metric: continuously available, varies with activities, relates to an individual's performance. What goal metrics meet these requirements?

Proposals for suitable goal metrics:

1) For sales people: "Sales" is a suitable metric. Although not all activities immediately result in sales and there are contributions from other workers, averaging sales over some time period (a month? a quarter?) provides decent statistics.

2) Work feedback sites such as "Rypple" and "tenXer" allow co-workers to contribute feedback that can be used as a goal metric. (Although one can argue that the feedback is, in effect, data to be correlated with a goal metric.)

3) More tantalizingly, consider *spare time*. Spare time is the difference between the time it takes to complete a task relative to the previous time. Spare time is continuously available, changes at the rate activities are

performed, and is influenced solely by the individual. The act of generating spare time is equivalent to increasing efficiency. Better organization and prioritization produce spare time. Spare time is a wildly lucrative goal metric for performing Time management design.

And what can be done with spare time? Why, more work, of course, by which I mean generating spare time. Or goofing off—let's not forget goofing off.

# Implementing real-time feedback and self-evaluation

Let's briefly review. When we started this chapter all we had were problems. Only a few pages later it seems all those problems have gone away. Are you still skeptical?

We have found productivity levers in work processes (that can be identified using Time management design). We have moved from analog to digital data to eliminate the stopwatch and have found suitable goal metrics.

The last thing to consider in the implementation of Time management design is real-time feedback. How do you do it? What does it look like?

The feedback function in Time management design, as we have seen uses correlation, C, as an error condition to "push" activities in the right direction, which requires a kind of real-time self-evaluation.

Typically everyone does some sort of evaluation of their work, and God knows other people do, too.  The intervals at which we are evaluated vary and some work websites, noted above, increase the immediacy of feedback to approach real time. Clearly, you are the only one in the position to do real-time feedback.

What does real-time self-evaluation look like? Imagine being able to listen to a voicemail message while you record it. Or consider a ballet dancer or karate master practicing in front of a mirror. Why a mirror? It's real-time feedback, of course.

The idea is to constantly and frequently be evaluating what you do. After a client meeting, ask yourself: "How could I have done that better?" After completing some task, ask yourself: "What is the impact relative to other things I could have done?"

Of course, you should try to be honest with yourself and avoid cognitive biases, to whatever degree possible. Objective thinking, tied to emotional detachment, is a skill that can be developed using Time management design. How do I know that? Well, I always end up with "INTJ" when I take the Myers-Briggs test.

# Dynamic to-do lists

- Comparison with to-do lists
- Time management design is a to-do list on steroids.

Another way to look at the implementation of real-time feedback is by comparing it with to-do lists. As most people are intimately familiar with to-do lists I feel I can safely dispense with discussion of their more technical nature. For simplicity, let us say you make a list and then check off the completed items. When you have finished checking off all the items, you throw out the list or make a new one.

Clearly, this is analogous to the way we work. Transform the to-do list task from a procedure to a process and TMD can be viewed as a "dynamic" to-do list: generating and checking-off activities while tracking a goal and varying tasks to push the goal higher. What I am proposing is working while correlating, identifying, and leveraging capacity improvements—checking-off dynamic to-do list items all in real time.

And thus, we have arrived at our working implementation of Time management design based on digital outputs representing the deliverable of activity and spare time as the goal metric. In this Brave New World, fractional outputs correlate with increasing or decreasing spare time to optimize percentage activities and outputs increase via the feedback process that identifies 80-20 Rule-type capacity improvements.

We introduced the subject by implying Time management design can be used to increase productivity by orders of magnitude. If you consider various alternatives, is it really surprising that we arrived at a self-optimizing scheme based on leverage?

- Practice offline
- Shorten the evaluation cycle

Like learning a new language, implementing Time management design does not come without practice. You can practice offline to ramp up your skills by shortening the evaluation cycle.

The following exercise will help: Write your job description. One month later, do it again. Six months later, do it again. This will help you reflect on what you do, what it is you *should* do, and how to reduce the gap.

The bits of Time management design that can be done "offline" are the same as those that should be done in real time: record outputs, vary them, track a goal, correlate the two, identify leveraging effects, squeeze-out spare time, and drive a goal higher.

# Job description design

- Generalizing outputs in terms of your job description
- time management -> results management

Let us look at a couple of modifications to Time management design for useful purposes. The first is a generalization of activities in your job description.

Write your job description in terms of functional blocks that contribute to a goal. For example, if your goal is sales, instead of tracking phone calls, e-mails sent, clients met, etc., lump them together in a block called: "Customer Relations." All administrative tasks go into another single category.

By combining activities based on common parts of your job description and applying the same methods (fractional analysis, correlation, and feedback) you can reduce or increase the parts of your "percentage job description" that contribute to your desired goals.

This illustrates that Time management design can be used not merely to optimize activities but the entire "what" of what you do. You could say that this procedure moves from time management to results management, optimizing your job and entire worth to the organization and ultimately, yourself.

# Time management design as comparator

- Apply Time management design to tasks, ideas, or strategies pairwise.

Another interesting modification to Time management design is to use it to compare issues, policies, or strategies and determine best practices or quantify wasteful activities. Compare, for example, productive work and administrative tasks, meetings versus everything else, or (for salespeople) customer contacts versus other stuff.

Throw the tactics to achieve strategy A in one block and strategy B in another. Comparing directly competing ideas or visions in a data-driven environment is objective and produces accurate results not based on hopes or wants.

# Last points to consider

Time management design is a tool that can increase your work capacity by orders of magnitude and optimize your worth to the organization. These are bold statements.

I will be the first to agree that what I have proposed is quite radical: a revamped way of work (that has a completely traditional way of work as its point of departure). For the remaining discussion let's consider why Time management design works—despite the radical parts.

# Chapter Four

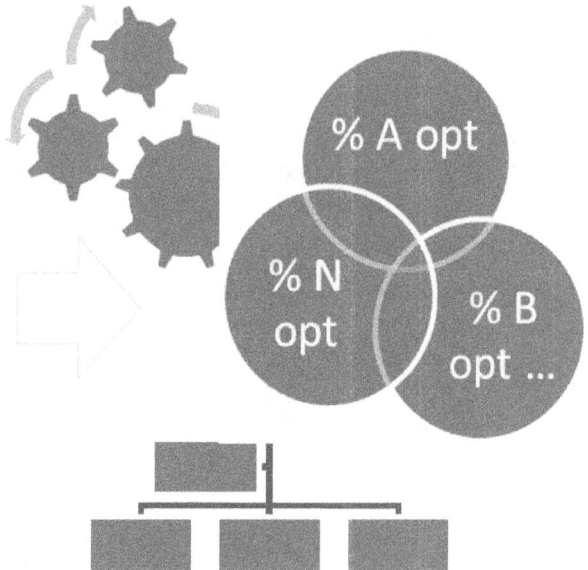

# Why Time management design works

# Why Time management design works

We have established the principles of Time management design, reviewed its implementation, and described alternate ways to use the tools to provide additional benefits. What remains apart from a cheery collection of stories detailing how people have used the tools to make themselves happier and more productive is a brief discussion about "Why Time management design works."

You see, Time management design principles are like gravity, they apply whether you believe in them or not. Let us look at some reasons why implementing Time management design can improve individual and organizational performance.

# Time management design is old-fashioned

Elements of Time management design exist even in the most arcane of business settings. There are few companies that do not use employee reviews, to-do lists, goal setting and tracking. Time management design is a way to frame these concepts from an enhanced perspective. By setting a new course based on the principles laid-out in this book, you will be working within the system while simultaneously bringing it down. Rather than anarchy, you obtain order.

Why?

Time management design improves your results orientation. The process concerns self-evaluation and control plus organizational awareness. It is about speeding up what you do and aligning it with corporate objectives (or changing them!). Time management design enhances all the good things about work— personal knowledge, creativity, productivity, openness, and exchange.

Many organizations are resistant to change, which is why there is always the tantalizing option of going undercover and using the techniques for your own benefit. If the organization is a mess, only the most stealthy, slippery work under the radar will net you the satisfaction you deserve.

# Quantitative techniques take people out of the problem

Good ideas deserve a way to be proven apart from the nonsense of office politics.

At its core, Time management design is mathematical and as devoid of emotion as the workplace is likely to get. The more data driven organizations become, the more open they will be to using analytical tools.

And since this is an inevitable occurrence in the evolution of business theory, as more and more companies tie their operations to metrics, you will be in the vanguard.

Imagine the feeling of well-being inherent in a workplace without tyrants, drama queens, yes men, and the people who blame you for their own mistakes while taking credit for your good ideas. It's an imaginary world, I agree, but one worth imagining.

# Good riddance!

Like the great Wizard of Oz, incompetent managers deserve to be unmasked.

I've worked for my share of clueless managers and know first-hand that they can make life as satisfying as living in a North Korean gulag. Any principle based on analytics is going to bring transparency to the workplace and expose these bunglers. Your quality of life is sure to improve when these jack-asses are handed a pink slip. Good riddance!

# How to deal with an annoying boss

If you have an incompetent boss, here is how to get him or her off your back.

Suggest they implement the techniques in this book! After chuckling at the thought of lowly you advising God-on-high, they will start to feel clammy as they realize what you are suggesting is at odds with a practice they hold most dear—acting impulsively on delusions of self-greatness.

Their tendency will be to shuffle you off in the direction of least resistance, minimizing contact, and banishing you to the farthest corner of their muddled brain as they go about their business of pushing a misguided agenda on others.

Or they could fire you.

# The design goal

The design goal is to make work easier via increasing efficiency and simplifying actions, eliminating waste and increasing the capacity of your tools.

If you consider that you want your job to be easier and that you can make your job easier, then what on earth is stopping you from making your job easier? Whatever that barrier is a thing to eliminate.

I have made myself unpopular at company meetings by asking, "How can we make this easier?" Business people (who want to be seen as "hard workers" with subordinates who "follow their example") simply do not want to hear this.

We have proposed spare time as a goal metric which is the most obvious workplace characteristic never mentioned. Tell people your goal is to generate spare time and they will assume your next position will be in the unemployment line. Yet, these are the same people whose goal it is to "look busy." They are simply "putting in their time" and would never share their real goals and motivations, immersed as they are in suspicion, insecurity, and lack of self-worth. Get thee behind me!

# A workers' manifesto

- These ideas are not so far from the mainstream.
- Both management and employees have a vested interest in pursuing Time Management design principles.

Although I have framed Time management design as a "Worker's Manifesto" in the sense that superior execution keeps the wolves at bay, there is within it a wealth of value for Management as well as workers. The concepts outlined here deserve a wide audience at different levels of the business organization.

For Human Resources: imagine a corps of self-evaluating employees who agree on the goals and actions taken to meet them and work at high levels of productivity because they are vested in their own decisions.

For Management: imagine savvy subordinates competing for your position and aligned with corporate objectives. Their work is characterized by transparency as they regularly produce accurate, data-driven reports.

For Upper Management: a tool for sacking Middle Management.

And the list goes on.

The task of implementing Time management design in the workplace is not only an investigative effort imbued with potential for change but also a creative endeavor. The mere conversation about goals and activities implies a meeting of the minds and hashing-out of ideas and shared values in a meritocratic environment among equals. Well, I wouldn't go that far. But, Time management design places people outside of the problem and allows employees to be empowered in the decision-making process. Carrying out Time management design in stealth fashion yields the side benefit of imagining yourself as the Man from Uncle or Perry the Platypus thwarting evildoers.

On a more serious note, as we wind down toward the ultimate task of saying farewell, my gratitude will be to those who take these ideas and run with them. I am vested in your experience and how implementing Time management design has made a difference. Since I am alone in my incubator, please let me know you are out there by visiting timemanagementdesign.com or dropping a line at feedback@timemanagement design.com.

As you read these words, if I have reached the status of Malcolm Gladwell, Jeffrey Gitomer or Seth Godin, then yours will enter a vat of never read e-mails and spam. On the other hand, if nobody you know has ever heard of Michael Kotas or Time management design, then chances are your e-mail will be read with interest as I plot my next move to free the proletariat (which concerns planning and reporting to connect past and future by annihilating the present, like the Hindu god Shiva.)

# Conclusion

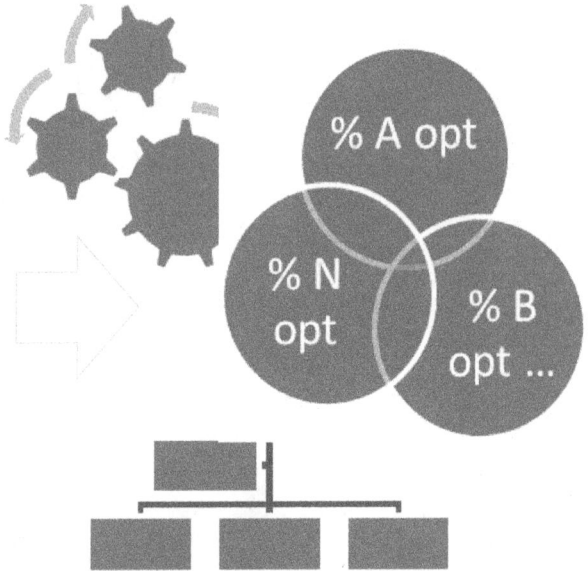

## Know thyself

# Know thyself

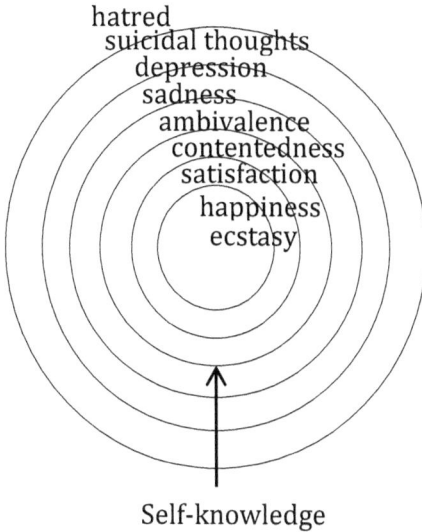

hatred
suicidal thoughts
depression
sadness
ambivalence
contentedness
satisfaction
happiness
ecstasy

Self-knowledge

I wrote this book to get the information out there and, truth be told, make some money. The person who has made it this far must see within the analytical self-evaluating model something of value. I have presented an organizing principle around which to make better decisions, an underlying theory of work optimization.

Normally, a book like this would include a chapter devoted to the success stories of people and organizations who have applied the techniques to achieve world-beating results. You probably realize that is not going to happen.

Truth be told, I have not shared these ideas with organizations or many individuals until now. My hope is that freethinkers will adopt these ideas based on their concept of utility. And my words to those utilitarians are these: *"Be the oil in the machine. Enjoy the satisfaction that comes with knowing what's going on."*

Self-knowledge is key to a successful life. Time management design, at its core, is about self-knowledge. Evaluating what you do, quantifying the results and making adjustments in order to improve what you are good at can all result in happier, healthier humans.

Can Time management design make you a better person? Probably not. A better worker? Indubitably, yes.

So go out there and seize the day! You have nothing to lose but your chains. While you are at it, please share with us your stories of pain and redemption, freedom and glory, or cold-blooded revenge.

Thank you and good luck, Neo. You are the one.

# Appendix 1: Summary of the method

- How to do Time management design, as described in the book *Time Management Design* by Michael Kotas

Step 1: Think about what you do, what you have to do, what you think you should do and what you want to do. Make a percentage activities chart showing, % A ini, % B ini, etc., the proportion of time it should take to do those things. Start recording outputs. Try to determine if the proportions you estimated are accurate.

Step 2: Vary % Activity A. Isolate the variation by subtracting from % A ini.

Step 3: Correlate with a goal metric. Use the correlation to "push" Percentage activity A to an optimum state. If the goal goes up when you do more, do more. If the goal goes down when you do more, do less.

Search for leverage by identifying things that drive the goal up; squeeze out spare time. Alternatively, use the technique to compare strategies, functional parts of your job description, etc.

Step 4: Visit TimeManagementDesign.com for the latest tips and ideas on optimizing your self-worth and salary.

# Appendix 2: Relationship between the correlation function and the goal metric

| 100% correlated | 0% correlated | -100% correlated |
|---|---|---|

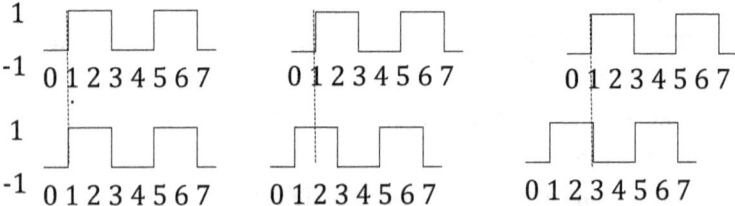

Following is a brief tutorial to reinforce some of the mathematics used in the book. First, to show that the mathematical operation, correlation, bears out what we understand correlation to mean. Above are three sets of time series, the pair on the left is 100 percent correlated, the middle 0 percent correlated, and the right mirror images are -100 percent uncorrelated.

In the text, we used the following form to mathematically express the correlation between two series.

$$C(R_A, G) = \frac{1}{T} \int_0^T R_A(t) * G(t) dt$$

Since the variables are distributed continuously in time, this is called the "continuous case." An equivalent expression can be used for the "discrete case" where the variables are discrete, digital values.

$$C(R_A, G) = \frac{1}{N} \sum_{i=0}^{N-1} R_A i * G i$$

Here, $R_A$ is Fractional output and G the Goal metric.

We apply this function to the time series above. The 100% correlated example, assuming $R_A$ is the top series and G the bottom, yields:

$R_A(0) * G(0)$ = -1 * -1 = 1
$R_A(1) * G(1)$ = 1 * 1 = 1
$R_A(2) * G(2)$ = 1 * 1 = 1
$R_A(3) * G(3)$ = -1 * -1 = 1
$R_A(4) * G(4)$ = -1 * -1 = 1
$R_A(5) * G(5)$ = 1 * 1 = 1
$R_A(6) * G(6)$ = 1 * 1 = 1
$R_A(7) * G(7)$ = -1 * -1 = 1

The sum is 8 and plugging the above values into the equation yields: $C(R_A, G) = \frac{1}{8} * 8 = 100\%$.

Similarly, for the uncorrelated case:

$R_A(0) * G(0)$ = -1 * 1 = -1
$R_A(1) * G(1)$ = 1 * 1 = 1
$R_A(2) * G(2)$ = 1 * -1 = -1
$R_A(3) * G(3)$ = -1 * -1 = 1
$R_A(4) * G(4)$ = -1 * 1 = -1
$R_A(5) * G(5)$ = 1 * 1 = 1

$R_A(6) * G(6) = 1 * -1 = -1$
$R_A(7) * G(7) = -1 * -1 = 1$

The sum is 0 and the value of C is $C(R_A, G) = \frac{1}{8} * 0 = 0\%$. Thus, the equation does indeed provide a measure of correlation.

Next, we look at the relationship between the correlation function and the goal metric. The illustration below shows a process in which % A ini = 25%. Increasing % A (left) results in positive fractional activity, reducing % A (right) results in negative $R_A$.

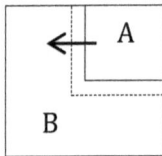
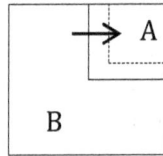

Positive R_A              Negative R_A

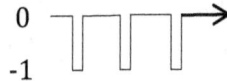

Note that whether G goes up with positive $R_A$ or goes down with negative G, the correlation is still positive and the % Activity area is too small.

G

R<sub>A</sub>

1
0
-1

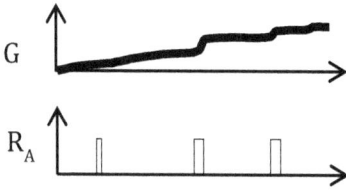

Goal goes up with
increasing % Activity

% Activity
area too small

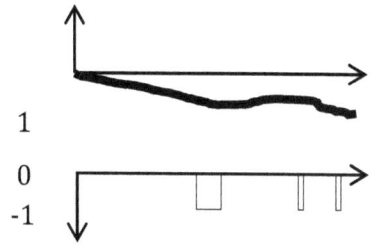

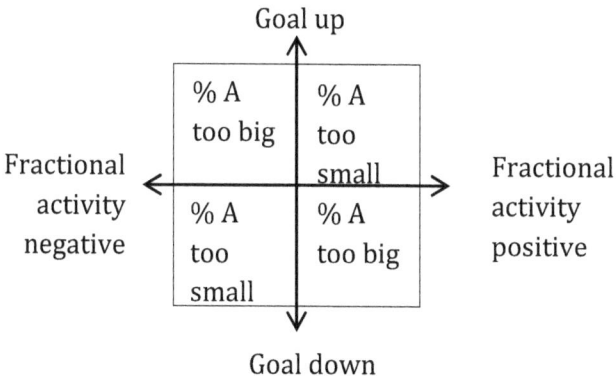

Goal goes down with
decreasing %
Activity

% Activity area
too small

Goal up

| | % A too big | % A too small |
| Fractional activity negative | | |
| | % A too small | % A too big |

Fractional activity positive

Goal down

We can repeat the exercise for the other two cases:
where the goal increases with negative R<sub>A</sub> and goes
down for positive R<sub>A</sub>. The four results are summarized
above. Although there are four cases of G vs. R<sub>A</sub>, there
are only 2 cases of C vs. R<sub>A</sub>, as was pointed out earlier—
C is the feedback signal.

The behavior of the correlation value vs. fractional activity depends on the shape of the goal metric vs. % Activity. The chart below shows the behavior for a few different cases. The important thing to note is that the correlation is zero where the goal is maximum, which renders it suitable for use as an "optimizer."

The optimum distribution of activities can be found by varying % A while tracking the goal using correlation. The correlation acts as an "error condition" that can be used dynamically to adjust a work process in real time.

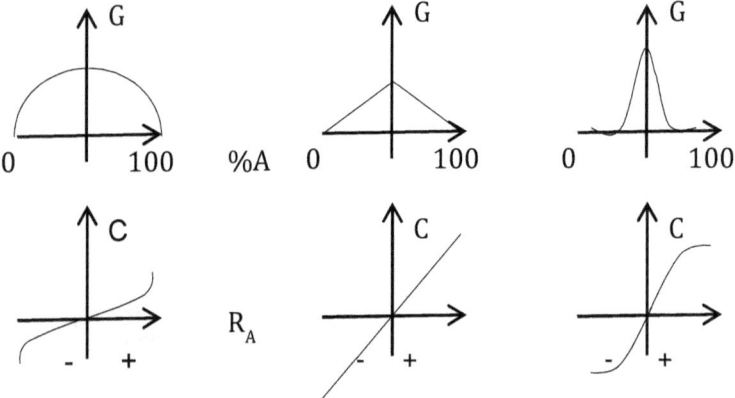

# About the author

Michael Kotas is a life hacker with a background in experimental fluid mechanics. He has spent his career in sales and marketing with small tech companies and specializes in the application of analytical techniques to business processes.